A SUMMARY OF QUADRAGESIMO ANNO OR ON RECONSTRUCTION OF THE SOCIAL ORDER

AN INTRODUCTION TO AND
PARAGRAPH-BY-PARAGRAPH SUMMARY
OF *QUADRAGESIMO ANNO* BY POPE PIUS XI

BY OMAR F. A. GUTIÉRREZ

No. 2 IN THE CATHOLIC SOCIAL TEACHING SERIES

For my Parents

Nihil Obstat
Rev. Matthew J. Gutowski, S.T.L.
Censor Librorum

Imprimatur
Most Reverend George J. Lucas
Archbishop of Omaha
August 11, 2020
Omaha, NE

Copyright © 2020 Omar F. A. Gutiérrez

No part of this book may be reproduced, stored on a retrieval system, or transmitted in any form or by any means, electronic, mechanical, photocopying, or otherwise, without the prior written permission of the author, except by a reviewer, who may quote brief passages in a review.

Excerpts from *Quadragesimo Anno*
are from the English translation.
Copyright © Libreria Editrice Vaticana.
Used by permission. All rights reserved.

ISBN-13: 978-1-7351641-2-0

Introduction

Catholic Social Teaching is a set of doctrines based on certain fundamental values. It provides principles for reflection, criteria for judgment, and guidelines for action. These principles, criteria, and guidelines have developed since the late nineteenth century in response to concrete historical circumstances, which have served as the backdrop for the teaching's pastoral approach.

In this second of a series of introductions to the social documents, we look at *Quadragesimo Anno* (1931) and to the intervening period between it and Pope Leo XIII's *Rerum Novarum* (1891), which began modern Catholic Social Teaching. In that time, much had changed in the world and the Church, and Pope Pius XI was calling for a restoration of a Catholic view of social life founded on Christian moral principles.

The Lion Librarian

Rerum Novarum was a watershed moment for the Church and for Her approach to the "social question," that is, the increasingly unjust situation that arose during industrialization whereby very few owners had massive amounts of wealth while the vast majority of workers lived in squalor. However, as important as the document was, Catholic Social Teaching could have ended right then and there. Pope Leo XIII was succeeded by Pope St. Pius X (1903–14), who issued no real development of social doctrine, though he certainly did not get in its way. He did encourage through his encyclical *Il Fermo Proposito* (1905) the Catholic Action movement as a way for Italian Catholics to participate as Christians in public matters of State and society. His hope was that lay Catholics might bring to bear in the Italian secular political environment what the Church's hierarchy could no longer demand. His very short encyclical *Singulari Quadam* (1912), referenced in *Quadragesimo Anno*, simply reiterates parts of Pope Leo's teaching regarding labor unions and gives "permission" to Catholics to be members of non-Catholic unions.

Pope Benedict XV (1914–22) succeeded St. Pius X and lived through the First World War. Ostracized by the victorious and losing nations for not having taken sides, he offered no advancement of the social teaching, perhaps because he was overwhelmed by the great tragedy of the war.

Then Achille Ratti was named Pope Pius XI (1922–39). A man of relatively humble background who had spent a good deal of his priestly life as an academic librarian, Ratti is described as being at once gentle, for instance in the way he used to personally care for the poor, while at the same time blunt, that is in the way he used to slam the tabletop when arguing. Whatever the case, all agree that the manner in which he addressed head-on the many dangerous threats to the Church that arose during his pontificate demonstrated remarkable courage.

He condemned both Italian Fascism for its totalitarianism and German Fascism for its racism.[1] He wrote an entire encyclical condemning Communism and its violations of human rights.[2] As he quelled the rise of a false ecumenism,[3] he reached out to Anglicans and Protestants in their common cause against the new atheistic threats to freedom and faith in the West. Recognizing the value of the Catholic Action movement, he vigorously encouraged the Church's hierarchy to support its lay members. He also saw to it that systems were put in place to spread and develop Catholic Action beyond the Italian model.

But all of this came after his erection of a new solemnity for the universal Church: the Solemnity of Christ the King. Promulgated in 1925, the encyclical *Quas Primas* argues that the social problems of the world are at their core problems of faith. He makes it clear that it would be an error to claim that Jesus Christ has no authority in the affairs of government or society. He is the Lord of all.[4] This is the beginning, then, of what is referred to as the "Social Kingship of Christ." It means that, as Catholics speak about and work toward social change, they should never forget that it is Christ Jesus who is the King, the true ruler, and the ultimate authority over how Catholics ought to effect society.

In all these ways, Pope Pius XI revealed himself to be much more than a simple librarian. He repeatedly defended the human dignity of persons of various races, classes, and faiths across the globe. During his pontificate, he was the lion protector of Western, Christian culture at a time when there were very few such voices willing to speak or allowed to.

The German Connection

In 1929, the whole world saw a collapse of financial institutions now known as the Great Depression. Deciding the Church needed to respond to this global crisis, Pope Pius XI chose the year 1931 to do so, exactly forty years[5] after the promulgation of *Rerum Novarum.* While Pope Leo XIII had expressed in Catholic language new answers to the problems of the industrial age, it was Pope Pius XI who recognized the genius of those answers, unpacked them, and built upon them to further develop the social teaching for his times. In doing so, he started the practice of popes assessing their moment, recalling previous teaching, and developing Catholic Social Teaching. Almost every pope after him would do exactly this.

Pope Pius XI's first task was to assess the roots of the Depression and to seek help in providing, as Pope Leo XIII did, practical answers that could at once advance the Gospel and help Catholics who were suffering. Unregulated markets and the greed of some of the very wealthy were blamed, in part, for the Great Depression. Others blamed the social programs erected to solve what was a correction in markets.[6] Whatever the case, as the economic troubles spread, Soviet Communism and lesser forms of Socialism offered themselves as the great solution to the world's troubles. Germans, who had witnessed crushing economic burdens placed on them by the victors of World War I, found themselves stuck between a version of Capitalism that in their eyes offered no hope of lifting the poor out of misery and atheistic Communism. It was German Jesuits at this time who pioneered a path forward that could at once criticize unbridled Capitalism while condemning both Communism and milder forms of Socialism. Their work caught the attention of Pope Pius XI.

The pope approached the Jesuit Superior General, Fr. Wlodimir Ledóchowski, SJ, for aid in writing this sequel to *Rerum Novarum*. The Superior General in turn tapped Fr. Oswald von Nell-Breuning, SJ, professor of moral theology at the University of Frankfurt. Well versed in the social teaching as it existed up to that point, he too felt he needed to consult outside voices. Without telling them why he was attending, Nell-Breuning started to participate in a discussion group headed by Fr. Gustav Gundlach, SJ. The group studied and discussed the writings of a Fr. Heinrich Pesch, SJ (d. 1926).

Having experienced both the rise of Socialism and the Catholic response of "Social Catholicism"[7] in Germany, Fr. Pesch condemned the extremes of laissez-faire Capitalism and Socialism's focus on class warfare and denial of private property rights. His masterpiece, *Teaching Guide to Economics*, which he spent most of his life writing, is a multivolume history of economic thought, a kind of *Summa Economica*. As a result of his years of dedicated study and thought, he would found what is known as Solidarist Economics. The word "solidarist" is a form of "solidarity," a central principle of Catholic Social Teaching, and refers to a unifying relationship amongst individuals that is deliberately chosen and that at once rejects radical individualism and radical collectivism.

This was the economic approach Fr. Gundlach championed, and in so doing, he become quite helpful to Fr. Nell-Breuning in drafting most of *Quadragesimo Anno* for Pope Pius XI.[8] Fr. Gundlach is said to have been particularly helpful in articulating the Principle of Subsidiarity, the regular call in the document for an end to class warfare, and the stated hope for a mutual cooperation of owners and laborers for the sake of the common good.

Major Themes

Quadragesimo Anno begins with praise for Pope Leo XIII, making it clear this document is an expansion and a development of *Rerum Novarum*. For many paragraphs, Pius recalls the teaching and wisdom of Pope Leo on the proper role of government and the importance of unions. We see in this document the first instance in official Catholic Social Teaching of the phrase "social justice." It should not be confused with contemporary notions.

Social justice as understood here is connected to St. Thomas Aquinas and the broader Scholastic tradition that developed over time.

According to St. Thomas Aquinas, justice can be divided into that which governs relations between individuals and relations between individuals and a community. The former is called "commutative justice." So, for instance, the fee one person may pay to another for the work of mowing a lawn is commutative justice. Each party receives something in return or "commutation," hence "commutative justice." The latter is called different things at different times. Aquinas uses "distributive justice" when referring to goods communally held by society that are then proportionally distributed to individuals. For instance, in a farming cooperative, all members of the co-op pay their dues and receive the same benefits from the co-op. Should the costs to the co-op rise or fall, then the dues will rise or fall proportionally on the members. However, there is also the obligation of an individual to advance and maintain the common good of the community. Aquinas refers to this as "general" or "legal justice." Yet, it is exactly this general or legal justice that is called "social justice" in *Quadragesimo Anno*, an example of which is provide below.[9]

The document also warns against the two extremes of "individualism" and "collectivism," the former expressed most often in Capitalism and the latter in Socialism. Regarding individualism, *Quadragesimo Anno* maintains the long-held Christian tradition that wealth, while not itself evil, can very well lead to a numbing of the conscience overrun by the passions. This results in a kind of self-interest that clouds the wealthy person's obligations to the common good and therefore social justice. Thus, States, to maintain social justice, must be involved in some way to regulate the free market. However, the harshest language in the encyclical is directed at Socialism, saying that it is fundamentally incompatible with Christian belief. Even milder forms of Socialism, which had reportedly abandoned class warfare and State ownership of all property, are rejected by the pope.

Regarding unions, *Quadragesimo Anno* reiterates Pope Leo XIII's support for workers to organize in order to secure their rights as laborers. However, it is also clear that unions must work in collaboration with the owners and managers of a business. It is possible, according to the encyclical, that unions can get too greedy and demand so much that it harms the business. Therefore, it also warns against unions becoming too large and political.

Two of the other major themes in the encyclical are just wage and access to private ownership of capital by laborers. A just wage is a matter of social justice because, without such a wage, families suffer and lose stability. Healthy families are needed for the maintenance of the common good. Therefore, under the virtue of social justice, employers are obliged to provide such a wage. Subsistent wages are a bare-minimum requirement for a just wage, but a truly just wage is one where the worker can, through frugality and self-discipline, put aside enough money to attain private property. In this way, the worker can better secure his or her finances and provide for the family in the future after his or her death. Again, this serves the common good and so meets the social-justice obligation of the business owner.

Finally, it is this document that articulates for the first time that foundational principle of Catholic Social Teaching: the Principle of Subsidiarity. The pope argues that higher orders of authority ought not take from lower orders of authority their right to meet their obligations themselves. So, for instance, the State ought not so regulate a business so that the business cannot itself meet its own obligations particular to its own community. The Latin word *subsidium* means "aid." Thus, the principle is directed toward subsidiary relationships wherein the higher order exists to help, not take over, the lower order's efforts to meet its obligations.

Christ the King

Quadragesimo Anno broke new ground in Catholic Social Teaching and provides some of the foundational language for it. However, the longer title of the document is "On the Reconstruction of the Social Order."[10] Much of this reconstruction has to do with the reconciliation that the Church seeks between the class of owners on one side and the class of laborers on the other. But the closing paragraphs of the document show that better social policy and conflict resolution are not at the heart of the reconstruction. Rather, the reconstruction of the social order requires a restoration of Christian moral theology.

As Pope Pius XI says, even the best public policies will never replace the need for a fraternal compassion founded on Christ's love. A union may work well at securing a just wage for its members, but it is also obliged to guard the souls of those same members, who need to be able to worship and work in a moral environment. Employers may pay a just wage, but they too have an obligation toward the spiritual life of their employees. Governments may do well to maintain the fulfillment of distributive and social justice, but they have a more fundamental obligation to allow for public religious practice. To strive for social justice, then, without care for the immortal soul of the individual, will inevitably result in the failure to achieve justice of any kind. Because no document from a pope should be taken in isolation from his other teaching, Pope Pius XI's teaching on the Social Kingship of Christ, that is the restoration of the preeminence of Jesus' authority in society, can be said to be a leitmotif that plays at times throughout this document.

Quadragesimo Anno was received well by the world, but the ability of the Church and the world to take up its teaching was severely hampered by the explosion of the Second World War; the dominance of ideologies like eugenics, which escaped any mention in this document; and the fact that the next pope, Pope Pius XII (1939–58), did not write a document advancing Catholic Social Teaching.[11] He would be the last pope to fail to do so.

Paragraph-by-Paragraph Summery

The student of the social teaching should always be encouraged to read the full text of the constitutive documents. Admittedly, some are easier to read than others. Pope Pius XI's style is readable. Still, there are several references that may be confusing to the reader, and long, Ciceronian sentences can be disorienting. The following paragraph-by-paragraph summary is meant only as a quick guide to aid reading the text itself. It is not meant as a total replacement for reading the original text, as it is not exhaustive of the wonderful teaching given by Pope Pius XI in this encyclical. Nevertheless, quotations from the official English translation of the text have been provided in order to convey more precisely the language and feeling of Pope Pius.

Introduction

1. It has been forty years since Pope Leo XIII's encyclical *Rerum Novarum*, and all Catholics want to remember it fittingly.

2. Pope Leo's previous encyclicals laid the groundwork for *Rerum* on subjects like the proper understanding of Church and State relations, obligations of Christian citizens, Socialism, and so on. However, *Rerum* was perfect for the time as it addressed "the social question."

3. By the end of the nineteenth century, the Industrial Revolution had created two classes whereby a small number enjoyed great benefits while the majority of laborers suffered under "wretched poverty."

4. Some of the wealthy considered the situation to be the natural result of the laws of economics. They argued that the plight of the poor laborer should be handled by charity. However, the reality was that the laborers "were barely enduring," and this caused some of them to attempt to undo the whole system. Others, led by their Christian faith, rejected such a drastic approach but did still advocate for significant and rapid change.

5. Many Catholics, priests, and laity, as they engaged in charitable work, agreed with this latter

position and concluded that the inequality could not be part of God's Providence.

6. Despite their sincerity in seeking answers to this problematic situation, they were considered suspect for their innovation by some and at the same time were criticized by others for not going far enough. As a result, "they were at a loss which way to turn."

7. Consequently experts, laborers, owners, everyone sought out the advice and aid of the Vicar of Christ, the pope.

8. The Holy Father Pope Leo XIII sought the advice of those many experts, laborers, and owners and determined that he must say something about the pain and suffering of so many. Thus, he chose to speak "in virtue of the Divine Teaching Office,"[12] not just to the Church but also to the whole world.

9. And so, on May 15, 1891, Pope Leo XIII, despite his age, spoke out and taught the world how to address these difficult questions.

10. You bishops know *Rerum Novarum*. You know how the illustrious Pontiff decried the suffering of workers in the face of immoral employers and unchecked greed. You know how he did not seek answers from Liberalism or Socialism.[13] The former proved it was not addressing the problem correctly, and the latter offered a solution that would have made matters worse for the poor.

11. Pope Leo XIII also understood that the Church is key to finding a proper solution to these problems since these matters involve foundational principles of moral reasoning and Divine Revelation. He, as the head of the Church, was duty bound to respond, and his response was that both the very wealthy and the laborers need to be in right relationship with each other.

12. The good pope's work was received well, not just by faithful members of the Church but even by those who, though far from the Church, worked on or considered the "social question."

13. Laborers were naturally quite joyous at having been defended by the Holy Father, as were all who lamented the condition of workers. So it is that *Rerum Novarum* has been held dear and, even in some places, commemorated on the anniversary.

14. However, not all received the document with such joy and love. Some, even some Catholics, found it disturbing and approached it with suspicion. These "slow of heart" disliked that it criticizes the dominance of Liberalism and knocks down various biases. Still others thought the teaching grand but unrealistic.

15. Consequently, as Catholics are coming into Rome on this fortieth anniversary of *Rerum Novarum*, in order to commemorate this great document, I feel it is appropriate for me to: (a) recall its benefits, (b) defend it against doubts and develop

its insights, and (c) with a mind to current problems, point a way out through "the Christian reform of morals."

I. Recalling the Benefits

16. Recalling all the benefits of the document would require a summation of the last forty years, which would be too long. They can be summed up through the three areas in which the pope desired to provide clarity.

What Can Be Expected from the Church

17. The first area is what ought to be expected from the Church, for, as Pope Leo writes in *Rerum Novarum*, the Church is tasked not just with theoretical instruction but also with morals and living morally, in this case in reference to laborers and their working conditions.

18. The Church allowed Her teaching to be widely spread for the sake of the common good. In fact, Pope Leo XIII and his successors proclaimed the truth in the concrete circumstances of the time, as did many bishops at their local levels.

19. As a result, scholars both clerical and lay have sought to authentically develop this "unchanged and unchangeable" teaching by applying it to the new circumstances that arise in different times and places.

20. Thus, "a true Catholic social science has arisen." This new science has not been stuck in the theoretical realm but rather is made manifest in new academic courses, in conferences,[14] study groups, and various publications.

21. This is not to say that the teaching has been limited to Catholic circles. It has spread into the minds and hearts of non-Catholics through periodicals, books, legislative bodies, and halls of justice.

22. Indeed, the international community, which sought to reform the world after World War I through international accords, adopted language and principles pertaining to laborers that matched those of Pope Leo XIII's work.

23. The Holy Father's teachings have thus spread widely and been utilized. They have raised up the laborer, whose numbers had increased as a result of industry but whose rightful place in society had not yet been realized. Along with so many efforts by the clergy, the Church has shown laborers their dignity, rights, and duties. They have become leaders of their communities.

24. As a result, economic security has been increased for laborers, not just through charitable works but also through, again with the help of the clergy, the foundation of organizations and cooperatives for various trades and types of employment.

What Can Be Expected from the State

25. The second area where *Rerum Novarum* helped is what could be expected from the State. Against Liberalism, the Holy Father teaches that the State cannot see itself as only a keeper of laws. Rather, it has an obligation to be a source by which individuals and the public as a whole can achieve wellbeing. Freedom is to be maintained, yes, but always with an eye to the common good. The State's duty is to watch over the community but particularly with care to "the weak and the poor." This is because the poor do not have the means to protect themselves. And since the working poor are so numerous, the State ought to care for them especially.

26. There were naturally some States that sought to care for the sufferings of their workers. But it is also true that, after *Rerum Novarum* was promulgated, many more governments sought policies to better care for the laborer.

27. The document even inspired individuals to advance those policies within democratic legislatures. In some cases, the very policies being voted on and enacted were devised and encouraged by members of the Catholic clergy.

28. In this way a new form of law and governance has arisen from the effort to protect the dignity of the laborer. This new area of legal and governmental interest addresses "the protection of life, health,

strength, family, homes, workshops, wages, and labor hazards, . . . with a special concern for women and children." Even though these new laws do not always match Pope Leo XIII's teaching, there is no doubt that their existence is owed to his document.

What Can Be Expected from the Labor Unions

29. The third area asks what aid could be expected from labor unions, which could be a cooperative of laborers or of laborers and employers. Here, the Holy Father spends a great deal of time explicating their "purpose, timeliness, rights, duties, and regulations."

30. His teaching was greatly needed, for many States, influenced as they were by Liberalism, not only ignored labor unions but also were openly hostile to them. Even among some Catholics, there was suspicion about such cooperatives because they smacked of Socialism.

31. For this reason, Pope Leo's rules governing right cooperation were key as they helped to quell some of these suspicions. But more than that, his teaching encouraged Christians to found unions based on Christian principles in opposition to the Socialists, who painted themselves as the sole defenders of the worker.

32. Pope Leo XIII's teaching makes clear that the labor union should be directed toward three goals: (a) a healthy body, (b) a healthy soul, and (c) an increasing private ownership of property. The most important is the healthy soul fed by religious worship and moral formation. This is the most important because, when piety and moral formation are in place, the mutual cooperation necessary to achieve the other two goals will be made easier.

33. Clergy and laity answered Pope Leo's call and sought to found these cooperatives. In doing so, they have produced truly Christian laborers who, inspired by their religious precepts, work not in opposition to others but in a spirit of communion for the benefit of the whole social order.

34. The goals laid out by the Holy Father were applied differently according to circumstances. In some places, all three goals were sought out by one cooperative. In other places, several different organizations were formed to address labor rights or economic aid or religious formation.

35. The latter option has been necessary in places where the laws, the economy, or bias against these teachings have kept Catholics from forming their own organizations. In these places, Catholics are unfortunately forced to join secular unions. Those unions should respect and support the conscience rights of Catholics. Local bishops should be aware of these unions and be sure that they adhere to the precautions laid down by Pope St. Pius X.[15] He

taught that in such cases there should be Catholic institutions to form union members in the religious and moral teachings of the Church.

36. It is thanks to Pope Leo's teaching that the number of unions have increased. And though too many workers find themselves in Socialist cooperatives, there are still many Catholic laborers who are defended by institutions founded upon the Christian principles of *Rerum Novarum*.

37. Beyond the work for industrial laborers, the teaching has fostered similar efforts on behalf of farmers and of middle-class workers, who also are in need of spiritual formation and economic aid.

38. Sadly, the formation of such cooperatives cannot be said to have taken place "among employers and managers of industry." The reason for this is not limited to resistance from individuals. Still, we hope for and believe we already see some movement in this area.

39. All these benefits demonstrate that the teaching of Pope Leo XIII was not just unrealistic thinking. Rather, they show that the good Pontiff drew from the Gospel a teaching that would help to truly heal the rift growing within humanity. The fruits mentioned above demonstrate the power of the teaching sown on good ground, and so they show that *Rerum Novarum* is "the *Magna Charta* upon which all Christian activity in the social field ought to be based." Those who disagree and ignore it

either "blaspheme" or lack understanding, or they are vicious in their lack of justice.

II. Regarding Doubts and Developments

40. At the same time, some doubts about the meaning of *Rerum Novarum* have resulted in controversy. Accordingly, we take the opportunity here to answer these doubts and misunderstandings.

41. Still, before we proceed, a principle that Pope Leo XIII lays out should be repeated: the Church is within Her rights to pronounce authoritatively on "social and economic matters." True, the Church is not an expert in all things, but the Church does have authority over "all things connected with the moral law."

42. While it is the case that morals and economics are two distinct fields, it is an error to claim that they are so distinct that they are not connected.[16] Economics does involve itself with the nature of finite goods and human action, but reason can tell us about the "individual and social nature of things and of men."

43. Finally, the moral law points us to the ultimate end of all human action. Thus, economic actions, like all human action, guided by morality, ought to be directed toward achieving that end, namely God Himself, "the supreme and inexhaustible Good."

On Private Property Simply

44. But now to the particulars, and here we begin with the right to private property, which the Socialists reject. Some have accused Pope Leo XIII and the Church of being in league with the rich against the worker, but this is most unjust.

45. The Church has never denied the "twofold character of ownership," which is both individual and social. Yes, individuals have a right to that which is necessary for their and their family's lives and flourishing, but God also desires that the goods of the earth be accessible to "the entire family of mankind." To accomplish this, there must be a certain order.

46. So the "twin rocks of shipwreck must be carefully avoided." The first is "individualism," which acknowledges private property but ignores the responsible public use of that property. The second is to ignore private ownership so as to fall into "collectivism." Failure is to crash into the "moral, juridical, and social modernism" of either of these extremes condemned in my encyclical *Ubi Arcano*.

47. To quell this controversy, we need to return to the principle of Pope Leo XIII: "the right to private property is distinct from its use." Commutative justice[17] forbids the distribution of property in such a way that might infringe on the right of another to acquire what is necessary for life and flourishing.

However, the oversight of this distribution must be a matter of virtue and not legality. What's more, the right to private property cannot automatically be rescinded because of "abuse or non-use."

48. Those should be commended, then, who seek to regulate the limited material goods in such a way as to secure broad societal use and preserve private property as the Church understands these. Those who so restrict ownership so that private property ceases to exist are in error.

49. Because there are individual and social aspects to private property, one must therefore take into account the common good as he or she considers the use of his or her property. And the State, enlightened by "the natural and divine law," can determine what is truly necessary for the common good. Still, history demonstrates that private property and its use have taken different forms. And the State ought not be arbitrary in executing its duties. For instance, the right to leave property to heirs "ought always to remain intact and inviolate." Therefore, it is "grossly unjust" to seize private wealth through such high taxation that they leave families with nothing. At the same time, the seizure of private property can in some cases be justified in the name of the common good, since God provides for all earthly goods for "the support of human life." This seizure, when carefully considered, is not an instance of the State weakening private-property rights but strengthening them.

50. For indeed, "Sacred Scripture and the Fathers of the Church" make absolutely clear the obligation of the wealthy to give from their excess through "almsgiving, beneficence, and munificence."[18]

51. Giving in such a way that creates jobs that produce truly valuable goods for society is an excellent example of "munificence."

52. Further, the tradition agrees that ownership is acquired by "occupancy of a thing not owned by any one and by labor." Truly, it is when one's labor changes an object for the better that he or she can say to have a claim on it.

On Private Property and Labor

53. Now, labor that is exacted on the property of others is a special case. Here Pope Leo XIII's teaching is most clear, namely that wealth is a result of the labor of workers. Everyone agrees and understands that those nations that have risen out of poverty did so thanks to the great toil and effort organized by some and executed by others. At the same time, it is also true that the materials upon which workers labor are provided by "God the Creator of all things." Therefore, unless one is working on his or her own property, the worker and the owner must be associated together, "for neither can produce anything without the other." It would be totally unjust for either the owners or the laborers to

keep only for themselves the fruits of what is produced by both.

54. For too long, the owner of property or capital has been able to keep too much, leaving so little left over for the laborer that he or she can hardly maintain or restore his or her life. That owners could treat laborers in this way has been widely, though not universally, held for a long time. These errors have been condemned not just by workers but also by many others.

55. At the other extreme, however, are those "intellectuals" who have argued that, save that which is necessary for the maintenance of equipment, laborers have a right to all the profits of a business that benefits from their labor. This is different from the Socialist argument, which claims that profits ought to redound to the State, but is even more dangerous.

56. In order to maintain justice and peace, then, capital and labor ought to heed the teaching of Pope Leo XIII that no matter how wealth is distributed, it all must serve "the common interests of all."

57. Not every distribution of wealth is such that it meets the desire of God. This is why Pope Leo spoke of making sure that this distribution safeguarded the common good or the "common advantage of all." This "law of social justice"[19] means, therefore, that no class can keep the other from sharing in the profit that comes of capital and

labor. Both the owner and the worker are in error if they seek to seize all wealth from the other. And to those who, in order to seize wealth from owners of capital, would use the words of St. Paul, that he who does not work shall not eat (cf. 2 Thes. 3:10), we say again they are in the wrong.

58. Therefore the distribution of created goods, which today is most lacking as there are a "few exceedingly rich" while there are an "unnumbered propertyless," must be conformed to the "norms of the common good, that is, social justice."

59. Help for the non-owning worker must be pursued, particularly since the pleading of Pope Leo XIII has been suppressed or ignored as "impracticable." Though there has been in some nations relative improvement in the lives of the poor since his time, with the global advance of industrialization, the sheer number of the poor has increased. And this is besides the situation of the low-wage farm laborer who lives often without any hope of ever owning land.

60. It is true that non-owning workers are not paupers, but the disparity in wealth between them and the very rich is nevertheless a clear sign that the goods of our age are not rightly distributed or available to all people.

61. This is why we must all endeavor to see that the "abundant fruits of production" are properly distributed among the wealthy and to the worker but

not so much that the laborer ceases to need to work, for "man is born to labor as a bird to fly." Rather, with frugality and prudence, the laborer ought to be able to own property, secure it, and, when he or she dies, provide some wealth for those left behind.

62. All this which Pope Leo taught we affirm and repeat. For if these goals are not pursued with purpose, we ought not be surprised when "agitators" disturb societies with revolution.

63. As was just said, the laborer must use frugality and prudence to secure property. But apart from the wage, what other possible means does he or she have to meet this end? Let us, then, address the question of wages.

On Just Wages

64. They are in error and misrepresent Pope Leo XIII's teaching who claim that working for wages is itself unjust and that all work must be done within a "partnership-contract."[20]

65. Still, while not absolutely necessary, it would be good if wage earners could join in partnerships so that they can, for instance, partly own the business, engage in profit sharing, or help manage the business.

66. Now, how much a laborer ought to be paid in order to meet justice must be determined using several factors and not just one.

67. Pope Leo XIII clearly condemns the view that a just wage can be calculated by one simple rule.[21]

68. So they are in error who claim that a hired worker can demand all the profits from the product that is the fruit of his or her labor. We have already explained why above.

69. Just as with ownership, there is a personal and a social aspect to labor. The laborer depends on a social body that can, for instance, produce the tools or protect the other means necessary for his or her work. What's more, the mutual cooperation of several entities is necessary for one's labor to bear fruit. If the social aspect of work is not considered, then accurately calculating a just wage is impossible.

70. And so, very important conclusions about the justice of wages can be drawn from this state of affairs in human labor.

71. First, the worker must be paid a wage from which he can adequately support his family. The other members of the family can contribute, as is helpful on a farm or in small workshops. However, child labor and forcing mothers to work outside the home is "grossly wrong." Mothers are intolerably abused when they are forced away from the training of their children in the home due to their husband's low wage. Thus, a father ought to be able to secure a wage to support his whole family. If this cannot be done, then "social justice demands" that changes occur until that is possible. Praise should go to those

who have devised ways to adjust wages according to the needs of an individual family and its burdens.

72. Second, the limitation on businesses must also be considered, "for it would be unjust to demand excessive wages" that may ruin a business. Now, if the business's lack of resources is due to poor management, this does not justify an inadequate wage for its workers. However, if the business suffers because of unjust burdens or immoral forms of competition forcing the business to sell products at an unjustly low price, then the fault lies with those responsible for the burden or the competition.

73. Third, employers and employees ought to work together with the help of the "public authority" to secure a just wage. If this cannot be done, then perhaps provisions should be made for the worker elsewhere, and the business should be shuttered. Whatever the path taken, Christian charity and kindness should prevail in discussing the future of the laborer and owner.

74. Finally, the justice of the wage should also be gauged by the degree to which it helps "public economic good." We have seen that the laborer should be paid enough so that, through frugality, he or she may set aside some wealth and secure some property. However, that one is able to find work is equally important. In truth, exceedingly low wages and unreasonably high wages can cause unemployment, which then hurts the wider economic good of a nation and the common good.

Social justice demands that wages not be too low or too high so that the maximum number of persons who desire and need to work are able to find it.

75. An appropriate median wage is good for society, as is the "right proportion in prices" of goods. With a proper balance between wages and prices and the needs of businesses, the economy can become like a single body where all parts are mutually helpful to the others and to the whole. This new "social economy" will result in each person having what he or she needs to flourish, thus securing for all a fuller life that "is not only no hindrance to virtue but helps it greatly."

III. The Christian Reform of Morals

76. What we have discussed so far, then, on property, wages, and the social order, is the beginning of a kind of restoration to which Pope Leo XIII devoted himself.

77. However, in order that this restoration move from theory to reality, "two things are especially necessary: reform of institutions and correction of morals."

On the Reformation of Intermediary Associations

78. About the former, we turn first to the State. This is not because the State can bring about all that is good but because the evils of our day have resulted

largely from an "individualism" that has destroyed the "rich social life which was once highly developed through associations of various kinds." As a result, there exists today in the minds of many "only individuals and the State." This harms the State because, with all the intermediary associations gone, the State has been burdened with expectations far beyond its ability.

79. It is true that because of many of the changes in society, small associations simply cannot do what they once did. Large associations are now required. But a "weighty principle . . . remains fixed and unshaken in social philosophy": just as it is wrong for one to forcibly take over from you what you can do for yourself, so it is wrong for higher orders of authority to take over what lower orders can do.[22] Every member of the society must aid the other and "never destroy and absorb them."

80. The State, then, should allow "subordinate groups" to handle small matters lest the State's attention become too distracted from those things that only the State can do. If it protects this "graduated order" and follows the "principle of 'subsidiary function,'" the State and all in society will be better off.

81. The first thing the State should see to is the abolition of hostility between the classes and the cooperation between industry and occupations.

82. The State must help to "re-establish" industries and specific occupations so as to move away from a society that organizes itself on the basis of class.

83. Laborers, as Pope Leo XIII explains, are not just a "commodity" to be bought and sold. They have human dignity. But currently, employers who hire and those who labor for hire are like two opponents at war. All understand that this war must end. But to do this, we must carve out a place in society separate from the question of class. For just as a small town is created because of the proximity of families, so, too, well-ordered associations can be created between persons of all classes but from within industries and within occupations.

84. St. Thomas Aquinas taught that order "is unity arising from the harmonious arrangement of many objects." Therefore, we similarly say that social order is achieved by unity arising from strong social bonds. The bond between employer and employee can arise out of their collaborative production of goods in an industry or through occupations that work toward the same goal.

85. The primary good toward which these industries and occupations should work is the common good of the nation. In some cases, when strife arises between employer and employee, it may be best that they deliberate a solution separately.

86. Just as Pope Leo XIII notes that all are free to choose the government that best suits them,

industries and occupations can likewise determine for themselves what their associations will look like in the end as they strive for the common good.

87. Members of the same industry or occupation can freely join with each other to form these associations or unions. They may organize their associations in a way that best benefits their members. The same is true for associations not connected to an industry or occupation. In all of them, they ought to be "in conformity with the mind of Christian social teaching."

88. Just as the opposition of the classes should be rejected as a foundation for society, so, also, we reject the notion that the economy should be "left to a free competition of forces. For from this source, as from a poisoned spring, have originated and spread all the errors of individualist economic thinking." Such an approach ignores the "social and moral character of economic life." In so doing, it argues that free competition will manage an economy "more perfectly" than any other human intervention. But the many evils of today that stem from radical individualism demonstrate that free competition cannot justly manage economic life unless it functions "within certain limits." Conversely, "the economic dictatorship" that abolishes free competition is not acceptable either. Therefore, individuals, associations, and the State must be permeated with "social justice and social charity" so as to create a "directing principle" for a "juridical and social order" that will manage the economy.

Most important is "social charity," which can be protected and encouraged by the State if the State is willing to, as we say above, adhere to subsidiary function.

89. And since nations depend on each other, international pacts of economic cooperation should be erected.

90. If the directing principle mentioned above is followed, then we can say of the social body what St. Paul says of the Church regarding Her unity (cf. Eph. 4:16).

91. Because various "syndicates and corporations" have been formed recently, it seems appropriate that this encyclical address these now.[23]

92. States have created a legally binding syndicate in some places, giving it the sole power to protect the rights of employers and employees. Though one can choose to be part of this syndicate or not, and though other associations that deal with labor are not barred from existing, all are forced to pay the "syndical dues and special assessments," and all are bound by the syndicate's labor agreements.

93. They represent both employers and employees, sometimes of the same industry, directing them toward common goals.

94. "Strikes and lock-outs are forbidden; if the parties cannot settle their dispute, public authority intervenes."

95. The advantages of this system are clear: classes are brought together, Socialism is tamped down, and "a special magistracy" is given authority to manage disagreements. However, there are some who worry about the State taking too much control instead of limiting itself to assisting subsidiary associations and/or of serving too particular political ends rather than a healthier social order.

96. In answer to this concern, it is first necessary to pray that God may bless all our efforts toward the common good. Second, the common good will be more readily secured the more those with "technical, occupational, and social knowledge and experience" participate in the reconstruction of the social order. More specifically, the common good needs the contributions of Catholics, properly formed by organizations like Catholic Action, who can apply the Church's teaching in this area.

97. None of this can be done without a restoration of morality. There was once a time when society was well ordered, though not perfect of course, and met the conditions necessary to bring about the above. But society either rejected moral teaching because people were too selfish to care for the suffering poor or because they were duped by "a false freedom and other errors" and so rejected any authority.

98. Therefore, having judged the current economic system as wanting and Socialism as worse, we need to root out these evils and seek out a "reform of morals."

99. Many changes have happened since Leo XIII in both areas.

On the Restoration of Morals: The Evils

100. Economies have changed quite a bit after our predecessor noted that the owners of capital and laborers cannot do without the other.

101. He did not seek to abolish the system of owners and laborers, as though it were evil in itself, but only to set it in right order. For it is against that order when owners seek only their own benefit, abuse laborers, ignore their social responsibilities and social justice, and reject the common good.

102. It is true that the industrialized world is not the only economic world. There are laborers in agriculture. They, too, are "being crushed with hardships," and we both address their plight.

103. But with the rise of industrialization, "the 'capitalist' economic regime" has spread wide and far.

104. Thus, our focus on this regime is truly a concern for all people, not just those in industrialized nations.

105. For not only is there a small number of persons with the majority of wealth, but also they wield a "despotic economic dictatorship" over the rest of society.

106. These control not just the wealth but also credit and lending. They control "the life-blood" of the economy.

107. This circumstance is a result of the unlimited freedom of competition that rewards a kind of survival of the fittest, that is, of the strongest and of those who ignore conscience.

108. This circumstance further results in "three kinds of conflict": (a) economic supremacy, (b) supremacy over the State so as to use its power, and (c) the conflict between States themselves.

109. The results of this "individualist spirit in economic life" you know only too well. They are: (a) self-destructive free competition, (b) economic dictatorship over a free market, (c) "unbridled . . .greed for gain", and (d) a universally cruel economic life.

Along with these evils is the problem of the State becoming overly involved in economic life so that, instead of being concerned primarily with the common good, it is concerned only with the wants and desires of the wealthy. In this way, the State becomes their slave. This results in two other evils: (a) "economic nationalism or even economic imperialism," and (b) "internationalism of finance or international imperialism."

110. We have addressed how to counter these evils here already but will mention them in brief again, using "Christian social philosophy" applied to the question of ownership and labor so as to avoid "individualism and collectivism": (a) private and social good of owners and laborers should be given equal weight, (b) their relations with each other should be governed by "commutative justice" supported by "Christian charity," (c) free competition should be allowed within limits set by the State, and (d) intermediary "public institutions" and individuals should all work toward the common good, that is, "social justice."

111. Regarding Socialism, it has changed since the time of Pope Leo XIII. It has split into two main branches, sometimes in opposition to itself but remaining "fundamentally contrary to Christian truth."

112. One branch has become what is called "Communism," which seeks two goals: class warfare and the end of private property. It pursues these goals openly and sometimes violently, and where it has won the day, it has wrought "cruelty and inhumanity," as evidenced in Europe and Asia.

Its antipathy toward the Church and God is also no secret. We certainly need not convince our flock of Communism's errors, but we must warn against those who refuse to see it as an imminent danger to society or refuse to address the circumstances or influences that make Communism attractive to some.

113. The other branch that remains with the name "Socialism" is less severe, as it rejects violence, class struggle, and the abolition of private property. Indeed, one might say that it strives for the very hopes of Christianity toward a just society.

114. If we reject the paradigm of class struggle, after all, we can engage in real dialogue and cooperation. And the right to private property having been acknowledged, we can focus on the errors of a "sovereignty over society" that concentrated wealth can produce. Such Socialism, which may rightly point out that certain kinds of ownership ought to be regulated by the State so as to avoid that sovereignty, can seem quite close to Christian principles.

115. This approach does not stand against Christianity, but it is not particular to Socialism either, so there is no need to be a Socialist to adopt it.

116. But let us not pretend that all Socialists who have rejected Communism have totally abandoned class struggle or the end of private property. They

have modified these ends, true. Consequently some ask, with those ends so modified, can Socialism finally be reconciled to Christianity, which might meet it "half-way"? This is "a vain hope"! Rather, let Christians show Socialists that their purported goals are best met through Christian faith and "the power of Christian charity."

117. But what if Socialism has totally abandoned those two errors? Can, then, a Catholic be a Socialist so long as no Christian teaching is compromised? This is a question with which many have come to us, and we say to them, no. As a doctrine, "historical fact," or movement, "Socialism . . . cannot be reconciled with the teachings of the Catholic Church because its concept of society itself is utterly foreign to Christian truth."

118. Christian doctrine insists that the human person was created to live under the authority of God and to worship Him so that, while living and working, he or she might find both earthly happiness and, in the end, eternal happiness. Socialism, however, ignores the transcendent and focuses only on "material advantage alone."

119. Socialists argue that economic activity, which is considered only in material terms, only has a social aspect. Therefore, the entire fruit of a person's labor must be subjected to society and its ends. The result is that the only important goal for such an economy is the highest efficiency in the production of material products. This is more important than

even freedom or the "higher goods of man." Those transcendent goods will not matter, they argue, because the greater production of material products will benefit society and individuals through "comforts and cultural developments." In the end, then, Socialism cannot be conceived without "excessive use of force" and false liberties unlike that "true social authority" that is granted by God.

120. While there may be some truth to Socialism, it is based on a vision of human social theory that is "irreconcilable with true Christianity." "No one can be at the same time a good Catholic and a true Socialist."

121. This must be applied then to how we approach a "new kind of socialist activity" that focuses on the training of children.

122. Since our encyclical on Christian education, *Divini Illius Magistri*, we have made it clear why the ends of such an education and this new socialist activity are not compatible with the faith. Subsequently, it is unwise to ignore this new effort as though it were not as dangerous as it is. "Liberalism" will lead to this Socialism, which will lead to "Bolshevism."[24]

123. Therefore, it is a great pain to witness Catholics leaving the faith for this Socialism and joining its ranks.

124. Seeking why this is the case, we hear the following: that the Church is on the side of the rich not the laborer. Thus, as a matter of self-preservation, they seek Socialism.

125. How painful it is that there are Catholics who are so dismissive or ignorant of that central teaching of Christianity that requires our love and care for all who suffer or, worse, who are so willing to abuse workers. We know there are some who hide behind false religion to ignore the plight of the worker. We will never cease to condemn them, for they are the reason for this perception against the Church. However, the whole history of the Church exposes this charge to be a lie that we care not for the abused worker. *Rerum Novarum* itself is proof against it.

126. Nevertheless, our pain cannot keep us from inviting our deceived children back to the Church and the faith, back to their Father's home and to their Mother who so strenuously seeks to reform society for "social justice and social charity." And we remind our children that they will never find the happiness and peace they seek without the Lord, who became poor, who seeks to comfort, and who will judge all according to their deeds.

On the Restoration of Morals: Christian Charity

127. Still, there is also a need to restore more broadly the Christian spirit in society, for without it, our work will be wasted.

128. This is why we have looked at the present moment and judged Communism and Socialism, no matter how modified, to be insufficient to the Gospel.

129. As in the words of Pope Leo XIII, only a "return to Christian life" in society can draw one's attention away from vice and up toward Heaven and so provide a true foundation for the restoration of the social order. Who can deny that our society needs this now?

130. Yes, the difficulties of the time are real, but what are they when compared to "the loss of souls"? So much of today's societal view toward economics is directed at distracting us from this point.

131. We shepherds, placed in authority by Christ, cannot ignore these dangers to souls. We must constantly think on how to help our flock, for what good is it that people come to better manage their wealth but lose their souls? What is the point of teaching them the principles above, if, in the end, they are swept away by greed?

132. The root of this temptation for our flock is disordered passion, which draws all toward "passing goods" instead of the eternal goods. It has been so since the Fall, but the present economic system has made it more intense a temptation. They have become numb to their consciences, which might warn them against doing evil so as to retain wealth

above all things. Indeed, easy riches or quick profits won in unregulated and risky markets can do damage to many. Laws passed to reduce risk to corporations have made matters worse, as corporations make decisions that may result in losses to "those whose savings they have undertaken to administer." And, of course, there are those who appeal to our baser instincts in order to profit from immorality.

133. Moral restraints administered by the State would have done much to negate these "enormous evils." But as industrialization rose with rationalism, which largely rejected universal moral norms, disordered passions aided by unjust economics resulted in the ruin of many lives.

134. As a result we see, to a degree unseen before, people ignoring their consciences for the purpose of amassing more wealth even at the expense of others. These lead others along the same path with their lavish lifestyles and their mocking of morals.

135. With owners behaving so poorly, the workers likewise did the same, especially since their managers treated them with so little humanity. The degree to which laborers, especially the young and women, were exposed to danger and immorality, the harm done to families, the barriers raised to the spiritual life and Sunday obligations, and the manner by which otherwise good people pursued wealth through evil deeds disturb the mind. Thus, work, which was for the betterment of the human person,

is now a tool of "perversion." "Dead matter comes forth from the factory ennobled, while men there are corrupted and degraded."

136. For this reason, we can never bring back the nobility of work without heeding the teachings of the Gospel. Yes, reason has a role in trying to restructure society for justice. However, this societal order for justice will be impossible without "the Divine plan," that is, that all things be directed back to God and to His will. And, yes, working for a living is fine, and increasing one's wealth in just ways is reasonable. But if God is kept in mind, and one's desire for riches is tempered by "Christian moderation," then labor and wealth-building will bring about a social order "within the bounds of equity and just distribution."

137. Still, charity must always "take a leading role." They are "completely deceived" who agitate for justice and ignore charity. True, charity is not the same as justice, which speaks to what is owed by right. But even if everyone received what was his or hers by right, and so received justice, charity is always necessary. "For justice alone can, if faithfully observed, remove the causes of social conflict but can never bring about union of minds and hearts." After all, the efforts for peace and justice must depend on this unity, for if it is lacking, even the best of laws and regulations will be useless, as we have seen. If the members of society believe themselves to be daughters and sons of the Father or, better, one "body in Christ," this will work toward

the common good. The wealthy owner will understand his or her obligations to the poor, and the laborer will abandon hatred toward the owner.

138. With a greater spread of the Gospel, we are confident that an authentic justice and peace will be realized in the world, a goal we have desired with you my brother bishops since the beginning of my pontificate. Praise, then, to you who have worked toward this, to all clergy, and to the laity, like those in the Catholic Action movement. Do not despair: we recognize the many difficulties and problems.

139. Let us all work hard to bring those tempted away by wealth and bitterness in this world back to the things eternal. You may find that this is easier than it seems as, at times, the desire of our hearts for the truth will result in change more readily.

140. Indeed, laborers are already responding well, particularly among young workers who are turning their colleagues into "comrades for Christ." And how wonderful are those leaders of workers groups who are working so diligently, at times at their own expense. Many youth are taking up the study of the "social problems with deeper interest" so as to better all of society.

141. This being the case, the next step is clear. With so many having lost the faith, we must "recruit and train . . . auxiliary soldiers of the Church" who will love "with a tender brotherly love."

142. And it is your responsibility, my brother bishops, and that of your clergy to "search diligently for these lay apostles both of workers and of employers, to select them with prudence, and to train and instruct them properly." This is a difficult work, but it must mean preparation through the study of "the social question" by persons willing to resist the extremes of either side through the "charity of Christ."

143. Those so chosen from the workers and employers for this "eminently priestly and apostolic duty" should instruct the young, found organizations, and lead study groups. The Spiritual Exercises are especially useful for "Workers' Retreats," for it will inspire authentic apostolic work for the "Kingdom of Christ."

144. The world needs these new soldiers, for while the Church shall prevail, as Our Lord promises, so many of Her children suffer. Hence, She must act.

145. So grave is the situation that everything must be tried, including diligent labor and "fervent and unremitting prayers to God."

146. The many enemies of the Church unite "in a single battle line" against the truth.

147. Therefore, the many efforts by the Church for "social and economic welfare as well as the fields of education and religion" ought not be undermined by too scattered an effort. So, under the unity of the

bishops, may we all work together toward the "Christian reconstruction of human society" begun by Pope Leo XIII "so that in all and above all Christ may reign."

148. That this may become so, many blessings to you all.

[1] *Non Abbiamo Bisognio* (1931) "On Catholic Action in Italy"; *Mit Brennender Sorge* (1937) "On the Church and the German Reich."

[2] *Divini Redemptoris* (1937) "On Atheistic Communism."

[3] *Mortalium Animos* (1928) "On Religious Unity"; the false ecumenism condemned was the notion that the Catholic Church should abandon Her own doctrines so as to maintain a kind of "unity" with Protestant denominations that find those doctrines false. Of course, this would have meant that the Catholic Church cease to be Catholic.

[4] Cf. *Quas Primas* #17.

[5] The words "quadragesimo anno" mean "on the fortieth year" or anniversary of *Rerum Novarum*.

[6] It is not the purpose of this text to weigh in on the truth or falsity of these assessments, only that these were and are at least two of the explanations offered for the cause of the Great Depression.

[7] "Social Catholicism" was the term coined by the great Bishop Wilhelm von Ketteler, Bishop of Mainz where Fr. Pesch was for a time stationed by the Society of Jesus. To learn more about Social Catholicism, cf. *A Summary of Rerum Novarum or On Capital and Labor*, the first book in this series.

[8] It is widely understood that Pope Pius XI wrote paragraphs ninety-one through ninety-six, as they pertained to matters specific to Italy. That popes use "ghost writers" for their teaching documents is not unusual.

[9] Cf. *Summa Theologiae*, IaIIae, Q.58 and Q.61, a.1.

[10] Ecclesial texts are often known by their Latin titles, which is

always the first few words of the text itself. So, *Rerum Novarum* means "revolutionary," and *Quadragesimo Anno* means "on the fortieth year." However, encyclicals often have an official title given by the pope that hints at the content but is lesser known.

[11] Pope Pius XII did have a number of radio messages in which he references the social teaching of his predecessors, and in 1941, he specifically speaks about *Rerum Novarum*. His contributions to the social teaching are more abstract, and so no encyclical by him will be included in this series.

[12] This is an important phrase as it means, according to Pope Pius XI, that Pope Leo XIII's *Rerum Novarum*, while not infallible, is still official Church teaching and not just speculative, pastoral musings.

[13] For the modern reader, it is important to note that "Liberalism" here refers not to the contemporary "progressivism" but more closely matches a kind of "libertarianism." The Latin word *libertas* means "freedom." Therefore, the liberals of Pope Pius XI's time argued for maximizing free markets by eliminating all government intervention in the economy.

[14] Catholic Social Teaching "weeks" or conferences do still take place in Europe, wherein local state, religious, economic, and labor leaders gather together to discuss socioeconomic and cultural situations in their local communities and seek to address them in collaboration using the Church's Social Teaching as a guide.

[15] Here the pope references Pope Pius X's 1912 document *Singulari Quadam*.

[16] This is an important point as there are contemporary complaints about Catholic Social Teaching by Catholics who claim that the Church has nothing to say about economics any

more than She has anything to say about geometry. However, Pope Pius XI is here arguing that economics is ultimately about human actions in society, and, in so far as it is, the Church's moral teaching tradition has something to say about it.

[17] In the context of this paragraph, Pope Pius XI means the commutative justice that ought to exist between an employer, who is buying labor, and a laborer, who is selling his or her labor.

[18] One such example from the Church Fathers is from St. Basil the Great, who said, "Now, someone who takes a man who is clothed and renders him naked would be termed a robber; but when someone fails to clothe the naked, while he is able to do this, is such a man deserving of any other appellation? The bread which you hold back belongs to the hungry; the coat, which you guard in your locked storage-chests, belongs to the naked; the footwear mouldering in your closet belongs to those without shoes. The silver that you keep hidden in a safe place belongs to the one in need. Thus, however many are those whom you could have provided for, so many are those whom you wrong." Homily on greed and the saying of Luke's Gospel: "I will pull down my barns and build bigger ones," §7 (PG 31, 276B–277A).

[19] This is the first use of the phrase "social justice" in all of the official social teaching documents of the Church, and it is limited to the idea that one class, for instance employers, may not keep from another class, workers, all the profits that come from a business.

[20] A "partnership-contract" is one where the employer and employees are coequal managers of the business.

[21] Cf. *Rerum Novarum* #44. There, Pope Leo XIII rejects the idea that the justice of a wage is determined simply by the fact that the laborer signed a contract.

[22] This is the first definition given of a central principle of Catholic Social Teaching known as the Principle of Subsidiarity. Pope Pius XI will go on to explain its meaning, but this is the full text which is often used as the definitive explanation of the principle: "Just as it is gravely wrong to take from individuals what they can accomplish by their own initiative and industry and give it to the community, so also it is an injustice and at the same time a grave evil and disturbance of right order to assign to greater and higher association what less and subordinate organizations can do."

[23] Paragraphs ninety-one through ninety-six were personally written by Pope Pius XI to respond to the realities in Italy of his time. Some short background here may be helpful. Throughout the 1920's, various factions grappling for power in Italy attempted to take advantage of the large influence of labor unions, referred to as "syndicates" from the influence of French movements of the time. Fascist syndicalism arose under Mussolini, with the result that national unions/syndicates were created by law. Constituting representatives from labor and employers, they were given the legal power to set labor rules nationally, and everyone paid dues to the syndicate. While individual laborers and employers could found and join their own unions, these groups had no legal power. Their members had to adhere to the labor laws set by the national syndicate. Paragraph ninety-one here is an introduction to this section. In paragraphs ninety-two through ninety-four, Pius XI is merely describing the situation in Italy. He is not recommending the system. In the remaining paragraphs, he begins to comment on the limitations of syndicates particularly as it pertains to the influence of Catholics in the national debate.

[24] This is the name not just of Communism in general but specifically of Russian or Soviet Communism founded and led by Vladimir Lenin.

www.ingramcontent.com/pod-product-compliance
Lightning Source LLC
Chambersburg PA
CBHW020608030426
42337CB00013B/1273